T0381199

I Have Something to Say

PW the Poet

AuthorHouse™
1663 Liberty Drive
Bloomington, IN 47403
www.authorhouse.com
Phone: 1 (800) 839-8640

Published by AuthorHouse: 07/07/2015

ISBN: 978-1-5049-0603-6 (sc)
ISBN: 978-1-5049-0604-3 (e)

Library of Congress Control Number: 2015905613

Print information available on the last page.

Any people depicted in stock imagery provided by Thinkstock are models,
and such images are being used for illustrative purposes only.
Certain stock imagery © Thinkstock.

This book is printed on acid-free paper.

Contents

I Have Something to Say

Words tumbling out, falling upon paper to tell a story,
Speaking to what's in a heart gifted from the Father.
It may not be what you want to hear, but it may speak to your heart.
It may not align with what you believe to be
true, but nevertheless I must speak.
Thoughts overflowing, unable to be contained,
must follow the destiny set in place.
A gift is not to be kept secret but to be shared; 'tis why the seed was planted.
'Tis why I have something to say.

Got

I awaken to the morning sun peaking through the window,
The sounds of birds singing their songs as the wind hums along.
Thoughts run through the bifurcation of a mind, speaking to what is.
Got my eyes to intellectualize the light shining on me.
Got my hands to grasp life, propelling me onward into the next realm of reality that is love.
Got my mouth to speak, telling of the secrets flowing from a heart bathed in grace.
Got my feet to walk into the destiny waiting, scripted by holy hands.
Got my ears to listen attentively, finding comfort in silence, letting words of wisdom change me.
Got each intricate part of me as one to become one with He who is.

Ask Not

You ask me to stop crying, my tears flowing like a river,
But you never question why, for it concerns you not.
Let not your jealousy show if I drive, live, wear what you believe is better than thine.
Did you ask or know about the roads I traveled, paved with pain?
The hours spent in despair, searching for an ending, looking for a beginning?
The hurt that burned a hole in my heart, slowing leaking out a lost soul?
Do not pose to believe that I think I walk ahead of you.
I am not more than you, for the sum of who I am Is subtracted from where I began,
Divided by my hopes and dreams,
Multiplied by God's love, His grace.
Let not your insecurities, your love not for self, seek to silence what I have to say.

Color not this blessed rainbow, exploding into colors,
Directed at me, because I said yes … to Him.

ALFC

In my attempt to understand, to comprehend what has transpired,
I could not help but put pen to paper and write:
In our determination, your determination to protect what we believed to be true,
Have we left joy, love, and peace in yesterday, closing the door on tomorrow?
Did you, did we do all that we could, or have we let self-righteousness distort our vision?
Are we saying, with hands folded in prayer, we heard the Father speak?
Saying this is the path thou shall take, but I was … silent.
Are we lost in the tranquility of His love, or have we evicted it from our hearts
While, within the enchanted garden of discontent, our souls cry out in pain?
Our faith is wavering, seeking inspiration, in search of love.
Has fear interceded, echoing words of mistrust, justifying decisions made?
For what transpired before has not found a resolution, a healing.
Are we frightened in believing we are honoring Him with
words spoken, but our hearts are far from Him?
Are we aware our humanness is screaming above all rationalization?
Would He be pleased with, would He condone the behavior
we have exhibited toward each other?
Did your bitterness, our bitterness, our need to be right, blind us to the hurt inflicted?
For tears flow, trying to erase disbelief, fueled by power that has infected a soul.
Wish I had a river, an ocean to sail away on,
Into a vastness filled with grace, bathed in His love,
Opening the door, leading to wisdom and mercy, transforming us to see.
For on a cross He hung, with nails in hands, in feet.
He had but one agenda … Love.

Barbara Walters

From a child's beginning,
Surrounded by many whose names were known for their celebrity status,
Not knowing in years to come her name would rise above theirs,
For the journey was just beginning.
For it gave rise to a passion in pursuit of a destiny-scripted prize,
Ignoring the whispers questioning the road chosen,
For closed minds and hearts placed her not along side them
But in a house surrounded by a white picket fence,
Never noticing the enthusiasm radiating from a given intellect.
Not deterred, believing every day was a new beginning to something more,

For invisible treasures were waiting to be found.

Not believed by the multitude dressed in suits of black who spoke with loud voices,
Wanting her to play but on their terms, not seeing the angels dancing among the clouds
Propelling her on this preordained destiny-filled journey.
We say thank you, for the courage, for the example, for writing a part of history,
Saying loud and clear that your dreams can be fulfilled, be reached.
Achievement is not an illusion but is fueled by grace,
Determination emanating from a heart in search of a dream … hers.
Questions and doubts were erased, giving way to the legacy left behind.

Now telling the story, no matter what was said or done, not their script,
Already set, not to be undone,
For they were not the authors of her destiny; heavenly sources say yes!

Beautiful Woman

I am the hopes and dreams of tomorrow.
I am transcending what was before and what is to come.
I am not limited to who or what it is said I am.
I am short, I am tall, eyes of brown, black, and blue.
I am painted browns of the rainbow and more.
I am a beautiful woman.
I am not the mistakes of my tomorrow or future.
I am poised to be and will become a person of worth.
Open your eyes to see the beauty of a soul in motion.
I am a daughter, a mother, a grandmother.
I am the resurrection of the consciousness, seeking to keep the identity of self that is I.
I am the addition of knowledge and the subtraction of an illusion.
For the relegation of learning leads to wisdom.
I am a beautiful woman.
I am a planted flower bathed in the moonlight,
Kissed by the morning dew.
I am falling rain flowing,
Ostracizing opinions but cultivating a mind.
I am relinquishing, I am surrendering all
That deprives me of the pure light
To know what is true, for I am possibilities believing.

I am a beautiful woman.
I am, we are redirecting paths to be chosen,
Propelling someone on to reach his or her full potential,
For someone saw the beauty within me ... us.
'Tis right that we, through actions that speak,
Lift up potentiated minds waiting to learn.
We are women empowered with wisdom, for life experiences say so.
Kissed by the love of the Father, bathed in His grace,
We are beautiful women. Do you not see?
Heavenly sources say yes!

Best Time to Love

You do not know how long until or when time will cease for you, for me, for us.
You do not know if tomorrow will be tomorrow
Or when the seas shall flow no more
Or when the stars that light up the heavens at night shall cease to shine.
Opportunity is before us; the best time to love is now.

Do not cry for me when I have taken my last breath, sung my last song, written my last note.

When time not spent, no shared moments, no giving of self.
Come, break bread with me, talk with me.
Learn what's in my heart, my soul,
For time moves swiftly, stopping for no one.
For the best time, the right time to love, is now.

True essence of love is to give of one's heart, one's time,
For just to give requires no act of love.
A tiny hello, a gentle touch backed by love, can light up the heavens,
Causing He who sits on a throne to smile.
Not asking for diamonds or pearls
But just that love be not only a part of your life but the most important part.
Do not let yourself be bankrupt.
The best time to love is today, right this minute, this second.

Do not pretend you do not see
The pain that eats away at my heart.
Do not ignore the tears that fall from my eyes
Behind close doors but obvious to all who can see, letting love be their guide.
Do not let the sand in the hourglass run out,
Crying wasted tears on those who can no longer speak but now are heaven bound.
It is the hour, it is the day; the best time to love is now.

Boston Marathon 2013

I thought it was dream, if not for screams piercing the air as smoke ascended,
Streets painted with red, flowing liquids escaping from the injured.
I thought it was dream, but it was not.
Self-realization led to the authentication,
For what my eyes beheld was true,
My tears falling, leaving a trail for whoever was searching.
Why, my soul screamed, but no answers could be heard above the sirens, taking those in need
To the waiting hands of those imparted with medical knowledge
While others searched for loved ones, praying with each step taken.
I cannot comprehend what lost soul was moved to commit such an act,
Whose mind was filled with such hatred directed at innocent human beings.
I am trying to assimilate, drowning in disbelief.
My heart is filled with pain.

I thought it was dream but only to find I had slipped into a nightmare.
Freedom running ahead, trying to escape those seeking to destroy it.
I cast my eyes downward but only to find a sea of injured.
Anger is seeping in, blurring my vision,
But I cannot, shall not let it penetrate my heart, my soul,
For then I fear I shall fall into darkness where they make their home,
Drowning in despair and hopelessness.
I choose instead to cast my eyes toward the heavens.
Father, we are in need.
They say, I've been told we are covered by your grace, your love, everlasting.
They say, I've been told no matter what we have done, you shall catch us.
Catch us now, hold us in thou arms on this day and those to come.
Release the pain, the hurt from hearts in turmoil to waiting peace.

Brain Culbertson

Fingers glide effortless across keys of ivory and black.
Beautiful sounds emanating, caressing each listening ear,
Reach in to unlock the secret door.
Opened by the melodies played, speaking to a soul,
Bathed in love, touched by heavenly hands.
Every emotion aroused, feelings that offer no explanation.
Tears falling on their own accord,
For the beauty of played notes cannot be denied.

Musical notes floating through the air.
No denying the passion, no denying the gift
Unknown to us, bathed in music at birth.
With first breath taken, it was so,
For the path was chosen, the destiny was determined.
Each stroke of the key awakens feelings lying dominant.
No words necessary, for his music speaks,
Releasing the desire that burns in our hearts.
I, we are in awe,
So we ask, we pray always let his heart be filled with music.

Carl Ray

In 1944, a child was born, stepping into a destiny scripted and written by holy hands,

Not void of pain, not void of tears, falling into love waiting.

Chasing dreams, becoming reality, walking into tomorrow.

Releasing the sun hiding behind a dark sky to shine.

Allowing embedded pain in a heart to be released to forgiveness.

To become, a husband, a father, an author, a mentor, an educator.

Leaving an imprint, a legacy that shall forever speak, but now
footsteps have been placed, stepping upon heavenly soil.

The rejoicing has begun. Do you not hear the laughter? Do you not see the
angels dancing among the clouds?

For the stories continue, just a different audience of a heavenly persuasion.

A soul has been set free to wander around wonderland ... calling it heaven.

Weep not too long for him, for you may miss the falling star
Or the gentle breeze caressing the leaves on the trees, saying, "Here am I."

Weep not too long, for you may miss the raindrops falling
Or the rainbow across the sky, finding not a pot of gold at its end but something familiar.

Weep not, for you may not hear the careless whisper at your ear saying, "I am with you Always, for memories infused with love shall not dissipate."

Weep not too long, for God was calling. He was waiting ... just for him ... calling it joy, for he has transcended, he is ... home.

Clifford Adams

Just a minute, just a second ago, a child was born, took a breath, cried.
Placed in loving arms waiting, kisses placed, counting toes, counting fingers.
Unaware of the possibilities, the roads to be traveled, stepping into a destiny scripted and
written by heavenly hands.
For a heart, a soul was infused with music, evident by the
angels seen dancing among the clouds.

Just a second, just a minute ago, this baby, this child held an instrument in hand.
Placed to waiting lips as musical notes floated in air, falling back down to caress listening ears.
Unlocking the door to the passion, seeking to fulfill a
dream running ahead of what was to come.
For on the other side of the rainbow, not a pot of gold to be found but … music, calling it joy.

Just a second ago, just a minute ago, with trombone in hand, he stood … playing.
Cannot forget that smile as the melodies danced above with each note played.
Cannot forget, for to him the word friend was not just a careless whisper.
I know he tried to ignore the angels beckoning, telling him, "This way … He is waiting."
I know he whispered, "My wife, my children, I love, I shall miss, but …"
He shall and is watching over.
Know that memories embedded with love cannot, shan't ever dissipate.
Just a second ago, he transcended, leaving behind all that was to what is.
Just a second, a minute ago, he was here, but now he is running
through a wonderland, calling it … heaven.

Dawn

Dawn is approaching, and tomorrow is searching for yesterday.
Someone turned the lights off, falling into darkness,
Trying to understand, asking why, crying out to listening ears.
Children being killed by children, taking up arms, trying to erase the pain,
Caught up in confusion, misdirected anger, saying, "I am here."
Officers succumbing to violence, upholding their duty to protect and serve.
Breath of life dissipating in air, the minute hand on the
clock off in the distance keeps on moving.
A woman, a mother lost a child, but it's buried in political agenda, angry voices shouting,
No one even noticing her tears for a child lost or feeling her pain.
Fear has taken root, everyone a suspect. Self-preservation is now a song we sing.
A virus given the name Ebola infiltrating this land we call America.
Rationalization is escaping,
Attempting to drag rights, screaming, saying, "Mine, not yours."

Someone turned the lights off, falling into darkness, hoping,
praying, this shall end soon … Father, are you there?

Dedicated to the Veterans

*Do you ever take a moment to think of those who fought in
wars but now lay silent, beneath the earth?
Does it ever cross your mind there are men/women fighting on
foreign soil, every second, every minute of the day?
Or do you say, "Not my country, not my fight," but freedom rings for you, because of them?
What angers you about their decision to protect, to serve?
Should we close our hearts, our minds to what is wrong in this
world, slowly dissolving into a vortex of darkness?*

Do you not tuck your child in each night, placing kisses of goodnight? They do not.
Do you not awaken in your bed, wrapped in the warmth? They do not.
Come Friday, will you partake in a dinner that is pleasing to the palate
While the sweet taste of wine travels down your throat? They will not.
Do you realize someone has left behind a husband, a wife, a
child, but yours are never far from your side?
Do you not think on nights when sleep is lost, with tears, they do not miss them?
Can you, can we on this Veterans Day bow our heads, pray that
the Father shall keep them wrapped in His loving arms?
If not, can you, can we at least say … thank you?

Dr. Maya Angelou

Words flowed like liquid as she put pen to paper and wrote,
Telling stories in rhyme like music floating out in air,
Awaking dominant senses dancing at the bifurcation of our minds
As we attempted to interpret, to understand what was so elegantly said, what was written.
Wanting to share the seed planted in a heart reaching out,
Never allowing her vision to be obstructed by agitated
thoughts, blocking the inner beauty of self,
Bathed in love gifted from the Father.
Took adversity, told a story, released a caged bird to dance in triumph.
A regal queen spreading wings to soar above the rest.
A voice that commanded attention, speaking with words of wisdom,
Thought provoking, penetrating through, causing us to question, to explore
possibilities, interrupting thought processes, leading to an awakening,
Leaving no doubt she was saturated with love from head to toe, kissed by the Father.
We shall miss this woman, this author, poet, mother, and friend.
But worry not, for a name says it all, for Angelou without ou is Angel, thus knowing the
way, Taking flight, making her way home to this place, this wonderland … heaven.

For Sandy Hook Elementary School

Our Father who art in heaven, we bow our heads this evening in prayer.
Our hearts are broken, our tears are falling, too many to count.
We are trying, we are praying, we are trying to comprehend, trying to understand.
Just babes beginning life, now placing footsteps, stepping upon heavenly shores.
Should not be, for we want to hear their laughter.
We want to see them run, but they now run to you.
We want to see them grow, from child into young man, into young woman.
We want to see them walk across the stage dressed in a cap and a gown.
This sadness, so hard to bear, I can hardly breathe.
I was told, it was said, safe in your arms they shall be, but our arms
want to hold them, kiss them goodnight once more.

Father, tonight someone is missing a wife, a husband, a father, a mother.
Can you stop by and tell us, tell them everything shall be all right?
Can you put back together hearts shattered into a thousand pieces?
Can you make them fit together once more?
Can you ease the pain that now cuts like a knife?
Can you help us, teach us how to love once again?
Will the tears ever stop flowing?
Will I ever be able to sleep again … through the night?
Reach your hands down from heaven, wrap us in thou loving arms tonight, for we need Thee.
We are seeking, we are asking, we are praying, tonight and each night to come.

Good Morning People

Let your feet touch the floor, move you to the shower. Brush your teeth, please. Grab some coffee or tea. The sun is shining but praying for rain. Make your way to your intended destination—work, gym, etc.—never forgetting, to all those who are saying no, not allowing you to leave your past in the past, reminding you with each breath taken how you used to be. There was, is, and shall always be someone saying yes, erasing every no, for His yes is bathed, saturated in love. Time to pass out a pink slip, an eviction notice, to all things, to those who cannot see the beauty of your transformation. In other words, time to say good-bye.

Hero

Someone said to put pen to paper and write.
A hero in nursing who has touched your life,
Someone who has made a difference.
To awaken each morning before the sun peaks over the horizon,
Feet touching the floor, shower, and is on the way.
Not knowing what awaits as hurried feet enter
This place, this building, where those who are ill are cared for.
Code blue echoing as the elevator rises.
Silently praying angels take speed; there is someone in need.

Evening has come, and one by one they come,
Asking, trusting, "Heal me. Let me breathe freely once more.
This pain I cannot bear. Shall I see tomorrow?"
Caring hands take control, and words of thank you follow.
May I, can you, when, why?
Questions overflow, fueled by anxiety.
But, one by one, an answer is provided.
Someone taps a shoulder. It is your turn. I shall watch over.

Someone said to put pen to paper and write.

Tell of things done, to make a difference.
To change an outcome, preventing those from placing feet stepping upon heavenly shores,
To returning home to loved ones.
Calling on the regulation of knowledge, to rectify impending outcome
As the midnight hour comes, and here am I,
Sometimes not heard by others. Father, be with us tonight,
Guide us, for this night we cannot do this without … you

Someone said to put pen to paper and write.
Telling of a hero that ends their name with the initials … RN.
But I cannot, for each one is a hero.
For in my lifetime, our lifetime
No matter the circumstances, each has made a difference.
Isn't this what matters?

Dedicated to Hurricane Sandy Victims

Tears flow from eyes of disbelief like falling rain,
For nowhere is there to lay my head on this night.
No dinner waiting to be eaten, no dishes to wash.
Cars reflecting the colors of the rainbow float pass eyes watching
As I search for a home no longer there,
My life's possessions carried away by the waters to places unknown.
Come talk to me, tell me what I must do.

Here am I in the darkness pondering what is to come of me … us.
Where do I start? Where do I begin?
Nothing do I now own except what clothes my body.
Questions unanswered run through a tired mind.
Dare I fall asleep in this spot, this place where I stand?
Is this a nightmare that I got lost in?
My tears draining a soul haunted forever more,
Images I cannot erase. Tell me, what must I do?
I shall wait patiently. Come talk to me.

Burning homes so ironic, for surrounded by flowing waters, they sit in the midst,
Yet obstacles block the paths of those courageously fighting.
Tell me there is hope, help me to believe again.
My child cries, but not a morsel of food have I.
Come talk to me. Do you hear me calling?
I want to see flowers blooming, reaching up to catch the sun
while their perfume fragrance scents the air.
I want to hear a melody carried by the wind, from children laughing at play.
Come talk to me, tell me the joy will return.
Should I bow my head in prayer?
Tell me what I must do, where to go.
Come talk to me. I shall be waiting. Tell me what I must do.

I Have

I have been silent, I have been crying, I have been praying.

I understand your anger, your frustrations, but am trying to conceptualize your actions.
Matches thrown, lit, to burn down buildings, moving
mobiles, to justify what you believe is right.
Removing, carrying off things not belonging to you, destroying property, not yours.
Whose life are you honoring or is it self-preservation?
For when the smoke dissipates and the sun rises, signifying the beginning of a new day,
It is your neighborhood that lies in destruction.
Do you not hear the voices carried through the time continuum?
Where are the businesses? Can, will someone do something?
But you burned it down, did you not?
Silent night, all is not right.

I have been sitting, I have been questioning, what if …
May I ask, just want to know, what frightened you about me?
They say it is because I reflect the browns of the rainbow, but internally I am you.
They said I had my hands up. I think I did.
Accounts of events have been told and retold through eyes seeing and words spoken by others
Till the truth is lost in distorted versions by those reporting, those writing.
But I say, yes, I did not uphold the law, but did I deserve to
place footsteps stepping upon heavenly shores?
May I ask, could you have not disarmed me by placing a bullet in my arm, my leg?

I heard it told someone called out, "I cannot breathe, I cannot breathe."
Someone videotaped it for all to see, I think. I believed the world heard my cries,
But it was as if no one heard because breath of life was escaping a body,
Knocking on heaven's door, calling angels.
Were you afraid? Were you frightened?
But a tighter grip I felt till I breathed no more.
I may not have been an upstanding citizen in your eyes,
But did I, should I have gotten my angel wings so soon?

I have been in thought, I have been praying.
No one awake, planning to take another's life.
Is it just possible, duty bound, trying to upload the law?
Maybe afraid, maybe feeling defiant, the person should not be because of the badge worn?
Maybe, but no one asked. Maybe so scared that a life ending that day could have been his?
Steel rounds released from a weapon not to be returned, reaching the intended target.
Realization of a decision from whence there is no return,
Although not believed a soul was changed for life.
A family in turmoil searching for safety, for made known by those
reporting, the street, the house where they dwelled.
Silent night, Father, bring back a holy night, for we need Thee.

I have cried, I have been sad,
For a mother of three off in a strange land, Abu Dhabi, teaching,
Imparting knowledge into those seeking.
But someone thought, believed that the regulation of knowledge is only for men.
In a mall, out shopping with twin boys, someone silences her voice forever.
They did not know her, not even her name, and sadly did not care.
Left bleeding on a bathroom floor, she stepped into the arms of waiting angels.
Silent night, holy night, when shall it end? For colors of the rainbow are beautiful
When we allow each to shine, to speak.
Silent night, the world is drowning, for love is in need of love,

For the death of two does not justify what has transpired,
Innocent only guilty because they were dressed in blue wearing badges … my soul weeps.

I have been praying, I have been crying, I have been hoping.
Father, who art in heaven, we need you to be the light through this darkness.
Fill our hearts with love. Make what is unjust just.
Let us see through your eyes of love, to erase hate running ahead, refusing to be caught.
Let us see, let us understand that change begins with us
So that nothing done becomes something done.
Father, may I ask, do not tarry, for yesterday has caught tomorrow,
And I hear whispered words carried by the wind, saying, "Too late."
Please change it to already done.

In Honor of the Men and Women in Armed Forces

The long weekend has begun, a party of sorts to some.
Barbecues, frolicking at the beach, relaxing, partaking in the spirits.
But let us not forget the reason, the why this holiday came to be.
To honor those who took up arms to defend, to give meaning to the word freedom.
Let us not forget how many mothers' tears have fallen to the words "I am sorry."
Let us not forget when the night falls, it is in our beds we
sleep, our pillows we lay our heads upon.
Can we remember that somewhere someone is overwhelmed by the disregard for human life
As they try to hide the tears falling, mixing with the rain,
Sending up a prayer to whoever is listening, "Please be with me, us"?
Can we remember we get to hug, to kiss our loved ones, but they may never see theirs ... again.
Can we remember they are seeing, they are experiencing things no human being ever should?
A mind so infiltrated with the debris of war that it can find no peace, no rest.
Losing arms, hands, feet, becoming disabled and yet trying not to let this be their label.
Can we set aside our self-righteousness, our politics on this day,
For it is not the why they should not have, but it is they did.
Do you think we can say, knowing it shan't be enough, can we just say ... thank you?

In Memory of Dr. Martin Luther King

In this word of idealism, self-preservation, war, hunger, pride, injustice,
Hatred for no reason except that the breath of life still flows through your body,
Are we living up to trying to be more than just existing?
Are we letting peace, freedom move us from yesterday to tomorrow,
Stepping into a resolution?
What would Martin say?
Would he be pleased with our efforts?
If no, would we be able to rationalize, explain why not?
Or would our words fall like ashes, saying nothing?
Did we forget the sacrifices, the hours spent marching in rain?
The bruises left behind on a face, an arm, a leg, a body?
The hours spent behind iron bars, looking out, wondering but knowing
On any given day, heaven would have a new angel.
Does love, does peace still stir your heart?
Do we lack the passion, the vision to effect a change, to be the change?

Does our love for others reflect all the colors of the rainbow?
Or do we not see a rainbow at all?
Do the words he spoke, lived by, have they found a home in your heart, your soul?
Are we listening to untruths fueled by misguided intentions?
For hands raised, guns pointed at each other—it is not the dream he visualized or spoke about.
Would he bow his head, tears falling into cupped hands, for the loss of a dream he held dear?
Are we trying to keep the dream alive or have we buried it
beneath conflict, disillusionment, anger, me not you?

Are we embracing the love he spoke about? Are we searching, looking, wanting a change?
Do we want, do we believe as he did by letting the pure light that is He guide us?
Does the legacy he left behind speak not for anything?
Should we all not ask, what would Martin say?
Breathe in, let it surround you, wake you up, rock you to sleep … love.

Jonathan Butler

As far as eyes could see, a sea of one room,
Yet this was a house, a home.
Children running wild, barely clothed,
Eating, sometimes not, sleeping, sometimes not.
An outsider in the land of their birth, my birth.
Painted browns of the rainbow kept me … us
From crossing over the rainbow into the land of lily white,
To sail away, to be free, to take a journey in search of more.
My tears falling into unrealized dreams,
But here am I.

Beauty of the melody drew me in, an avenue of escape.
Applause, money, food to eat, but not I.
Superficial words rang untrue,
Invisible, yet I stood for all eyes to see.
Just wanted to hear, just wanted to feel … love.
To seek an escape, medicine of delight, release me.
But in all my determination, why hovered in the atmosphere,
Eating away at a soul wanting a resolution,
Crying waterless tears to ease a heart searching,
But here am I.

Not known to me but a heaven-sent stranger
To show the way, to redirect a lost soul that was I,
Telling stories about a king who loved … me.
But I thought He only cared for those
Painted lily white, with eyes of blue.
Strange words, strange fruit, for who should love me?
Haunted by colors of brown, deemed inhuman.

Living life but not, let it rain
For now over the rainbow, not a pot of gold
But love exploding into colors, repainting that which was lily white.
I have come to know, to understand, to see
A life given to save a life ... mine, incomprehensible love.
Blessed am I.

Journey to Win

I am relinquishing the accumulation of what was not.
I am transforming from where I started,
Optimistic, determined, redirecting my path.
I am turning around, opening my eyes, my heart
To words permeating a soul to the possibilities.
Speaking to forgiveness, changing what was.
No music, but I have a song to sing,
For I am on a journey to win.
No longer apprehensive, for emptied out am I.
Now filled with He who is, and I just want more,
For my ending should be painted with a newness,
Awakening the hidden mystery of what is to come,
For I am on a journey to win.
Perfect I am not, faithful not always,
But the authentication of His words has erased uncertainty,
Saying the journey to win is no longer elusive.
Blessed am I.

Ken Ford

Resting on collar bone, this instrument of string,
With bow in hand, propelling downward, fluid-like strokes,
Eliciting sweet, tantalizing sounds, hypnotizing us with the seductiveness
As musical notes float in air, pulling us in to savor the sound.
Intense sensual movements, passion oozing with each stroke, each step
Taking our breath away, a crescendo of joyous rapture releasing the gift given,
Making a soul come alive, taking us on a journey,
Becoming one with this instrument of string,
Articulating unspoken desires, the quintessence of violinists.
We say merci, gracias, and thank you.

Ladies and Gents

The sun is about to peak as the night curtain falls, signifying the start of a new day, calling it the past, so let's go, people. Wake up, open up the window, throw out discontent. Replace it with happiness. You're alive, are you not? Toss out anger, for joy is just around the corner. Dry your tears, for you are perfection created by holy hands. Kiss good-bye, say good-bye to those who seek to step, get in the way of your light, shining upon you, blocking blessings, because they have lost, ignored, cannot find theirs. Step into this new day, see the possibilities waiting, those knocking with your name, stamped and spelled out with love, with grace, because He says so. Let's go, people. Brush your teeth, wash your face, your body, grab your coffee, your tea, let your reflection in the mirror reveal the you that you were intended to be, not who others want, think, told, but who He says you are.

Late

Late one winter day, a stranger entered my world.

Not sure how, not sure why, past the I do spoken, past the I love you.

Bloodied and bruised, I picked myself up only to be knocked down again.

Late one spring day morning,, you trampled my heart, ignored my screams

Stole my soul, shattered my dreams, turned my hopes into ashes, burned by your spoken words.

You did not like my dress, my hair, but I … apologized.

My reflection in the mirror says it was not enough.

Late one summer day before the sun set,

My silence interrupted by your voice raised in anger, calling my name.

Will today be the day that I take my last breath?

Early one fall day, an awakening, heard a voice say no more … the voice was mine.

Time to step out of the darkness into the light.

Courage emanating from every fallen tear, every bruise, every broken bone,

For I was determined to rewrite my story and not let you be the author,

For in the arms of angels I shall not be until He says so.

Marcus Miller

Musical notes floating in air, surrounding listening ears
As a father's hands glided across keys of ivory.
The lessons had begun, a son purely captivated.
Before the sun rose up over majestic mountains, standing,
Of dreams dreamed, searching for his reality.
Emerged drowning, for music was calling his name.
With pen to paper, musical notes appearing, words exploding into songs.
For with each breath he took, each step,
A heart overflowing, releasing the passion,
Knocking on destiny's door, scripted and written by heavenly hands.

Guitar in hand, strumming … bringing life to the silent strings,
Making them speak, sing.
Betraying a gift given, kissed by the Father.
Intoxicating sounds floating in the atmosphere
To dwell there in symmetry, cruising.
Angels could be seen dancing among the clouds.
Flowers in dew kissed meadows, blooming in brilliance,
For the sounds echoing stirred souls listening,
From this person, this man, that is he.

Not our imagination drifting on a melody played.
Harmonies, qualities caressing our senses.
Feet moving on their own accord to the rhythmic beat.
No matter how you add, subtract, multiple, or divide it,
Just as there are counted stars across the heavens,
Just as day becomes night, blessed is he, for the view through our eyes says yes!
May the gift given continue to breathe, speak, sing, play … music.
And may you hear whispered words carried upon wings of angels,
Falling down from heavenly shores, saying,
"I am with you always" … nothing but love.

Nigerian Girls

You do not know me, nor I you, but I am worth this interruption,
For I think you will understand, for I am a mother, just like you.
But somewhere between despair and daylight, with tears on my pillow,
A painted canvas of disbelief stands, showing the silhouette of her face.
A child, my child I carried in my womb, safe from all things wrong.
Now subjected to brutality, fueled by an erroneous misconception that she is to be assimilated.
Understanding is elusive, for one is man, a woman, both human beings.

You do not know me, for I am a thousand miles away across oceans, across mountains,
Frantically searching for an ending to this pain,
Not asking for money but just a moment in time … yours.
For something deep within will not relinquish, will not surrender,
Even though my heart has been shattered into a thousand pieces.
A soul, my soul will not rest, for I believe, I am asking,
Can you bow your head in prayer? Will you do that for me … us?
Can you ask, can you pray that girls are released back into their mothers' waiting arms?
I know you do not know me, and we may not speak the same language.
Calling all angels. Please take flight. Deliver these prayers this night.

Our House

To dwell within this house built from nothing to become something.
Now standing stately, each room designed with care, rising from a desire of want.
A dream realized from design to reality, this house was built.
From the pouring of the thick, gray liquid to lay a foundation,
To the walls rising out of nails, wooden boards, and more,
To the windows hung, to visualize views not seen before,
Letting the moonlit night enter in, to the counting of the stars across the heavens,
To the doors, opening to a welcoming knock, this place, this house ... now ours.

A new beginnings of sorts, for something beautiful shall
grow in this place, this house ... this home.
Making memories, to share, to love, to walk side by side into destiny's open door.
Stepping into its corridors, searching, holding onto, releasing what is to be kept and is not.
For the sand in the hourglass has emptied out and found not
a pot of gold at rainbow's end but ... a home.
It has been said, it has been told that a house does not, cannot be ... a home.
It is those that dwell within, letting love overflow into each spoken word, each task at hand.
A refuge, escaping from the noise, the intrusion, seeking to
change the meaning of the word ... family.

As we stand in the midst of this house, this home,
We silently whisper words, hoping the curtail of the wind will
propel them onward to the shores of heaven.
We ask that on days of dark, please provide a light to redirect our steps.
Let there be serenity, a deep awareness of knowing we have been blessed.
Whatever is to come, to be, let this house always be a ... home.
But above all ... let love remain till time's end.

Pastor Hurmon

From the time you took your first breath, your first step,
You were the miracle letting my love take control,
Touched by my grace, exploding into mercy,
Stepping out on faith to behold the glory of I,
Propelled onward by love into a destiny waiting,
Scripted and written for you by holy hands,
My desire to draw you close … to Me.

A source of strength for the test before thee.
Change not a heart filled with a divine spirit.
Footsteps across the time continuum guided by my grace,
With wisdom waiting on the other side of rolling hills of green.
Instilling my light in a heart, waiting for its season.
Weathering obstacles, stepping out.
Reflecting colors of a rainbow, infused with that which is I.

Love how you stand in my word, speak my word,
Reaching out to all, people trying to find a way,
Pulled in by your joy, your enthusiasm,
Trying to awaken sleeping souls to my abundant love,
To be made over by grace interceding and faith saying yes.
In the midst am I waiting. The door is open.
Words of music to my ears, I am changing, I am trying.

My son, you have arrived at your intended purpose.
So glad I am your hiding place,
For the task before thee is made easy.
In you I am pleased, I say … well done, nothing but love.

Dedicated to People of Philippines

You do not know me or my name.
I do not look like you or even speak your language,
But I am asking, I am hoping that you hear these words I speak.
We may be oceans apart, but hear my heart.
I arose barely alive, dug myself out of debris. Now I search for family.
A storm, a typhoon swept through my country, my home,
Bringing winds, destroying everything in its path.
Waters washing away all we owned, all we loved.
As far as my eyes can see, there is nothing left standing.
Lifeless bodies everywhere as a mother holds a baby in her arms.
Cannot stop the tears as they mix with the rain wetting my checks.
Not sure where I will lay my head tonight.
Not sure what or if I shall eat this morning, this afternoon, even tonight.
Do not know where to find drinkable water to quench my thirst.

I know you do not know my name, but can I, may I ask you to pray?
Some say He is not, but I have to believe, I must believe He is,
For my soul is dying. There has to be something greater than me … than us,
For when I look up in the starlit sky, it speaks to so much more.
Can you ask Him to make His presence known?
Let His grace fall on me, on us, to change the circumstances that surround us.
Can you ask Him to come soon? Will you pray for me, for us?

Serenity Garden

No more fallen fruit from the tree of life, not fully grown.
No chance to dream or step into a destiny waiting.
No opportunities to move through the seasons,
To change an unknown to a known,
To write a name in an open book waiting, calling it history.
Painted faces of brown, should not we be brothers?
All the hopes and promises lost to death waiting.
Ancestors from beyond cry out.
All the marching, the beatings, the tears for naught.
It is time for a change.

No more unnatural cessation of life.
No more watching red liquid flow from lifeless bodies
While tears falling like rain are embedded in pain, never ending,
Attempting to erase the hurt, sinking into darkness.
No more drowning in our sorrows; it is time for a change.
Lifting up my voice, our voices, angels take flight.
Father, do you hear me … us?
Tell me, tell us what to do, what roads to take.
Peace we seek, peace we ask for, guided by your grace,
Bathed in Thou mercy, stepping out on faith.
It is time for a change.

Until time speaks with an answer
Heard over majestic mountains standing,
Waters of blue flowing,
Carried upon the wings of angels,
Let us seek serenity in the garden.
Let the fragrance of the roses, the daffodils dance with the breeze,
Scenting the air, letting us know there is beauty within.
Let's feed it with love, avoiding the insanity of a lost soul.
Let us not take any more last steps or breath of life giving.
It is time for a change. Heavenly sources say yes!

They Say

They say I am a made-up story, just a fairytale.
If so, in the presence of danger without a resolution,
When sickness invades your body, making itself at home,
When the winds blow, the rain falls, destroying everything in its path,
When the churches are filled in the aftermath of tragedy,
When the tears will not cease because the pain is eating a hole in your heart,
Why do you call? Why do you whisper my name?
Why are you praying? Is it because you thought no one was listening?
If I am just a fairytale, why are you looking for, seeking comfort
from this make-believe person you say I am?
What makes you think, believe you are the only beings that exist?
For in the vastness of the universe, there are many secrets, but I am not one of them,
For your fairytale ending has been, was rewritten by love.

This Is Our Country

Brought here unwillingly across waters of blue.
Through the silence of the night, ships sailed.
Oars moved, flowing waters from depths of ocean blue,
To reach intended destination of strange beginnings, strange land.
Words tumbling out, falling, void of understanding.
Now today, not looking back but not forgetting.
Words heard across avenues of discontent.
No matter the justification or rationalization,
For the ship has come and gone. Here am I,
Reflecting every color of the rainbow.
Who are you to say, who am I to say,
This is not your country, not mine but ours.

Dreams locked away open by the key of hope,
Moved by passion to be more than just the definition of a given name.
Accumulation of all owned I carried, optimistic for change,
Idealism manifesting itself into freedom,
Chasing dreams, wanting more, looking for a resting place,
Hoping to be more than what your eyes could see.
My hair is too short, too long, too curly, too black, too blonde.
The language I speak is disturbing to your aura.
The clothes I wear, the food I eat, how I dance, my music,
Leave you wondering, am I a strange being from a distant star?
You did not know my story, nor did you ask.
Left a country in turmoil, searching for peace.
Night sky like light of day from exploding gunfire in air.
Took what I knew, cooked, sewed, cleaned, to make a life,
For the home of the free is where I wanted to be.
This is not my country, this is not your country, this is our country.

Words flow easily to insult the intelligence of the many.
Promises never to be kept, for others seek to oppose,
For purposes only lost to self-gratification, saying nothing.
Handshakes over spirits flowing, not concerned for those
Who lay their heads upon beds without pillows
Or call dinner the leftovers from bins filled with more than just what is not edible.
Closing doors of higher learning, but yet you question our intelligence.
Words falling like ashes colored in absurdity.
For the regulation of funds to be spent, there is no resolution found.
Like children bickering over things the other wants,
Telling stories, full of unintentional desires for self-preservation.
Self-assured. the erroneous conception is now authenticated
By the division of those searching for truth … America.
This is not your country, this is our country.

A lady stands, arm reaching up, words ringing out across the time continuum.
Give me your tired, your poor, your huddled masses.
Above raised voices of discontentment trying to stipulate, we say we are here.
Just over the horizon, around the corner of despair, a voice can be heard.
Who changed the words? For I know one nation under God.
Who changed the words? For I know we the people.
Who changed the words? For I know with liberty and justice for all.
Who changed the words? For I know all men are created equal.
For I thought it said endowed by their creator, not you, not me ... but He who is.
This is not your country, this is not my country ... for this is our country.

Tyler Perry

Must not let another sun rise or sun set. Must surrender to what is true.
You are, you have become the quintessence of ubiquitous.

Must not make a mind unavailable to the thoughts reaching out to speak
That who, what you do is dictated by who He is.

Cannot deny a soul, a heart bathed in love streaming down from heavenly shores … that is you.
Unwilling to change a path despite the noise from others speaking.
A collection of opinions falling like ashes … remaining silent.
For on the other side of a rainbow, a unique entity … grace
with faith in tow, reaching out to love.

So sorry a car was a place you called home, but it left the door open
To resilience, transforming thoughts into something advocating a change.
So sorry life for a moment in time offered no resolutions, leaving you drowning in despair,
Leading to an answer that a life must be terminated.
For who would miss, who would love … you?
But whispered words of a heavenly nature carried by the wind said … "I shall, I do."

My heart aches for a childhood interrupted by the cruelty of life.
My hand reaches back into the time continuum to wipe away each fallen tear,
But forgiveness carried on the wings of angels has infiltrated a soul kissed by the Father's love.

Thank you for your perseverance, giving birth to a dream instilled in your heart,
Dancing to the music played by mercy, by grace.
Thanks for the laughter allowing us to forget the tears, the pain for a moment in time,
To see beyond our vision, blurred by what did not always align with what was true.
Thanks for being an example to emulate, to repaint the rainbow of those seeking to be more,
Turning no into yes.
For eyes can see falling raindrops in air reflecting the sunlight, a prism of brilliant colors,
Telling us you are, you have become the raindrops in our lives,
Teaching us to see all the colors of the rainbow and to shine.
It shan't be enough, but I say, we say merci, grazie, gracias, and thank you.

We Shall Miss You

The past is behind us, the present is before us.
A new journey to take, a different road,
Drawn toward what is to be.
A new favor sweetened by life's destiny.
A decision made, an answer.
We shall miss you.

A family in tears,
Not related by the blood that flows through our bodies
But by a simple occurrence,
A shared place of work.
Bonded by compassion and understanding
For those who not by choice but needed
The knowledge, the skill, the experience,
To move someone closer
Where pain and despair do not live
To a place called home.

A quiet assurance,
Kindness without request,
For he knew, he saw
What was to be done
For those without a voice
Lying at times, just one breath away to an angel call.
A gentleman to the end
Speaks to honor, speaks to a mother,
Speaks to a soul bathed in grace.
We shall miss you.

But for now, we have decided to wipe away our tears,
For your destiny is your destiny.
We have decided to wish you well,
For life was meant to live.
We have decided to let you go
Even though there will be an empty spot in our hearts.
We have decided to let you know
That the friendship will remain like a constant star.
But what is more important, we have decided to ask the heavenly Father
To use the stars, the moon to guide you,
The angels to watch over,
And our heads bowed in prayer to pray for you,
For you will always be a part of our family.

When

When the noise of life chases you beyond where you should be,
When pain seems to bury you in sorrow,
When tears drown a soul seeking,
When light cannot find the way through the darkness,
When sleep comes knocking but is not heard,
When what is said leads to no resolution,
When all your tomorrows are erased by yesterday,
When a heart wants to believe,
Why not let Him write His name on your future, your past, your present?
Why not let His loving arms hold you, rock you into a destiny kissed by His grace, His mercy?
Nothing to lose but something to gain … a blessing,
For He gave His all just for you … calling it love.

Whoopi Goldberg

A crown of braids adorns her head, falling to frame a face
Known not to just a few but millions.
A smile that lights up for all to see,
Inviting those who choose to stop and experience the beauty within.
A soul who took roads not always aligning with what was true.
Medicine of delight gave an escape into places unseen,
Searching for, looking for that which was she.
Learned experiences gave birth to who we have come to know and love.
A gift given, a gift used, to bring laughter to those who at times
Only knew sadness, evident by the trail of dried tears,
Never knowing the joy that was given in that moment.
Forgetting all that was before, we say thank you.
The love of a mother who spoke into her life, words so clear.
Do not let them take your joy.

Do not let them define who you are and should be.
Do not let them rewrite your destiny, for it has already been written.

To guide along life's chosen path, waiting for the circle to be completed,
Sometimes not clear, sometimes not understood.
For words spoken, words written cut like a knife.
Tears flowed in the dark of night into cupped hands.
A hurt only known to a heart and soul that was hers,
But strength gave way to another day, another hour, another minute,
To redirect, to take a step down another path.
No answer to the question heard, for no stones were thrown,
For He knows my heart, my soul.
No regrets, for I am who I am and shall forever be Whoopi Goldberg,
And to your surprise, not mine, He loves me.

Dedicated to Firefighters in Yarnell, Arizona

Here we are asking why but echoing back ... nothing.
Here are we drenched in disbelief, waiting for someone to say
They have been found, they are safe, but only silence.
Father, here we are requesting release from hearts laden with pain.
Unanswered questions running with tears, seeking a resolution to grief,
Trying to hold on with each breath taken, our cup runneth over.
There was so much life left to be lived in those who have taken leave of this earth.
There are children waiting to be kissed goodnight, missing a father, a mother.
But in the arms of angels, they are now making their way home to You.
Father, hold us on this day.

We are attempting to understand, we are hoping, we are praying.
Upon wings of angels, deliver these spoken words to those you have called home.
We thank you with each bated breath taken, with each step we take, each song we sing,
For a courageous act, not knowing that your desire to help
Would lead you to open the door leading to heavenly shores.
We shall miss your smiles, your laughter, wishing our tears
Could build a stairway leading you back home once more.
We shall never forget you, for love does not.
Amazing grace, how sweet the sound, wrap us in thy arms this second, this hour,
To move us through the storm, for lost without you we shall be.
Here we are asking, Father, hold us this hour, this day, and always.

You Say

You say you cannot understand me, but I am speaking.
My clothes, my food, my music seem to ostracize me from being a part your society.
I reflect painted colors of the rainbow, but this disturbs you.
You know not my story, nor does it concern you.
I seek to be more than I am, but this does not align with your truth.
I am not a created nightmare of your hopes, your dreams.
I seek to be more than I am, more than I was.
Traveled seas of waters flowing, landing on shores of freedom ringing,
Across borders guarded, for America was calling.
Left behind buried tears from a life deemed inhuman,
Afraid to close my eyes at night, even in light of day.
Your leftovers from one day, a meal for the week, just for me.
Compassion obscured by the belief that I do not belong here,
Yet here am I, yet this does not speak to your heart.

I thought it said, "We the people." Am I not … people?
Bombarded with stories told, searching for, describing me,
painting a picture with words of untruth.
Placing pen to paper to disclaim what was said, what was written.
My thoughts lost as if burned, becoming ashes falling, leaving behind opinions,
Becoming sacred words spoken,
Describing this me I am supposed to be but am not.
I am a person of worth, I am trying, I am learning.
For I see, I understand, I am colors exploding into this land we call America.
I am the resurrection of a consciousness seeking to keep an identity,
Founded upon, "one nation under God."
But you say I do not belong. Yet here am I.

About the Author

PW The Poet has been writing poetry since junior high school. She has achieved many of her goals in life, but it has been her desire to have her poetry published, even if that means selling just one copy. That goal has now changed to sharing with the world the words gifted from the Father. It is His desire, so it is hers too. A gift given is not meant to be held hostage but to be sprinkled on others, and perhaps it can effect a change. PW The Poet lives in sunny California, which she loves. She has worked in the medical field for over thirty-seven years. One of her joys in life is to travel; she especially loves visiting places she has only read about.

About the Book

Events occur that may touch our lives, our hearts, leaving us questioning, searching for ways to express our feelings. This book contains words gifted to me from a heavenly source. The words have come alive, on paper, for all to visualize, to read, to maybe say what others could not. It speaks to joy, to sorrow, the tragedies in life that cause tears to fall in the silence of the night. It is a reflection into a soul searching, hoping that there are still possibilities leading to that which we all seek and desire … love.

Printed in the United States
By Bookmasters